KU-737-043

YOUR PLAYER PROFILE

SHOOT!
THE VOICE OF FOOTBALL
EST 1969

DRAW PLAYER PHOTO ABOVE

NAME:

AGE:

POSITION:

COUNTRY:

TOP SKILL:

RATING: ★ ★ ★ ★ ★

FAVOURITE TEAM:

FAVOURITE PLAYER:

KIT BAG

The first thing you will need to get started is a football kit. Pick your perfect style from the rack below or have a go at designing your own.

HOME?

AWAY?

SHIN PADS

BOOTS

DESIGN YOUR OWN

DRIBBLING SKILLS

MATCHDAY BINGO

NUTMEG

Grab a friend and go head-to-head to find out who can win all three points in Matchday Bingo. A fun game that means you can watch even more football! It does not get better than that!

CORNER KICK

HOW TO PLAY:

1. Cut out your bingo cards – if you don't want to cut up your Annual, photocopy the cards or scan and print.

2. Choose a bingo card each and watch a Premier League football match (or any with VAR!). If something written on your bingo card happens during the game, then cross out that box.

3. Keep watching until someone gets a line (three boxes in a row, either down, across or diagonally – they all count!).

4. If you want to carry on, keep watching until someone gets as close as possible to a full house – that's crossing off every single box on the card.

CARD 1

FREE KICK	RED CARD	NUTMEG
DEFLECTED SHOT	HANDBALL	SLIDE TACKLE
AWAY TEAM GOAL	LONG THROW	DIVING SAVE

CARD 2

CORNER KICK	YELLOW CARD	VAR USED
WOODWORK STRUCK	SUBSTITUTION	HEADED GOAL
'KEEPER PUNCHES BALL	HOME TEAM GOAL	PENALTY

DIVING SAVE

STAR SPELLER

The Premier League attracts some of the biggest – and longest – names in world football, but how well do you know them? Fill in these missing player surnames and see if you're a Premier League star speller...

RA _ _ F _ _ D (MAN UTD)

_ OU _ _ K (WEST HAM)

S _ _ _ H (LIVERPOOL)

HO _ _ JE _ G (SPURS)

CA _ _ WE _ L (NORWICH)

_ Z _ (CRYSTAL PALACE)

SM _ TH _ _ _ E (ARSENAL)

M _ _ _ EZ (MAN CITY)

A _ PIL _ C _ _ TA (CHELSEA)

CA _ _ _ RT- _ E _ IN (EVERTON)

I _ _ _ NAC _ O (LEICESTER)

Answers on page 76

SO YOU THINK YOU KNOW...
PHIL FODEN?

Everyone knows Phil Foden. The Man City ace has catapulted himself into the footballing stratosphere as one of the planet's greatest talents. Show us how much you really know about the England wonderkid by taking on these true or false questions.

1 Foden scored his first England goal against Denmark.

TRUE ☐ FALSE ☐

2 Foden passed his driving test first time, aged 17.

TRUE ☐ FALSE ☐

3 Foden is a boyhood Man City fan.

TRUE ☐ FALSE ☐

4 Foden has two cats named Kevin and Sergio.

TRUE ☐ FALSE ☐

5 Foden is Man City's youngest ever Champions League goalscorer.

TRUE ☐ FALSE ☐

Answers on page 76

6 Foden is a FIFA Under-17 World Cup winner.

TRUE ☐ FALSE ☐

7 Foden was born and raised in London.

TRUE ☐ FALSE ☐

8 Foden's dad is a Manchester United fan.

TRUE ☐ FALSE ☐

9 Foden has had the same haircut for his entire life.

TRUE ☐ FALSE ☐

10 Pep Guardiola called Foden the 'most, most, most talented player' he has ever seen.

TRUE ☐ FALSE ☐

STAR STAT!
Foden won 3 Premier League titles by the age 20.

HOW DID YOU SCORE?

0-2 F'oh-dear: **Your Foden knowledge needs Phil-ing in!**

3-6 Foden Fan: **Not bad at all – good work!**

7-10 King of the Phil: **You're a Foden superstar!**

YOAN VALAT/EPA-EFE/Shutterstock

Leeds United star Patrick Bamford has made his own way to the top-end of the Premier League goalscoring charts. Under the expert guidance of Marcelo Bielsa, the English striker has helped propel Yorkshire's sleeping giants out of the Championship and back where they rightfully belong – at England's elite level for the first time since 2004. But Bamford's journey has been anything but straightforward. Before joining Leeds in 2018, the goal-getter had played for nine clubs in just seven years – many of them loan spells. Now truly at home at Elland Road, the forward talks about his footballing journey, scoring in the Premier League and playing Bielsa-ball...

PAT
ATTACK

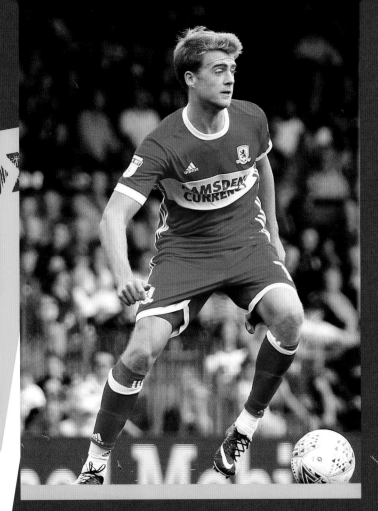

FACT FILE

NAME: PATRICK BAMFORD
DOB: 5.09.1993 — GRANTHAM, ENGLAND
POSITION: STRIKER
CLUBS: NOTTINGHAM FOREST, CHELSEA, MK DONS, DERBY COUNTY, CRYSTAL PALACE, NORWICH CITY, BURNLEY, MIDDLESBROUGH, LEEDS UNITED

Q: Can you explain the difference between the step up in quality from the Championship to the Premier League?

A: It's weird because the Championship is actually more physical - every ball is a fight ball. The Premier League is a bit more about intelligence. You'll have defenders who read the game a lot better, so rather than be physical they'll just step in and nick the ball. You have to be mentally in touch with the game the whole time, you can't shut off at all. Technically you have to be very sound as the opposition will pounce on any mistakes.

Q: How did it feel to score 17 goals in Leeds United's first season back in the Premier League?

A: I didn't really set myself too many targets. I said to myself, if I can get into double figures that's a decent season being a new Premier League team and it being my first real stint as a Premier League striker. Once I reached 10 goals quickly, I just wanted to push on then.

Q: Do you think Leeds' all-action, high-tempo style helped the team adapt to the Premier League quickly?

A: I think so. We're quite an expansive team in terms of the way we play and we're very fit. It helps with creating chances and you have a freedom on the pitch. Although we know what our individual jobs are, we have the freedom to use our ability and almost improvise on the pitch.

Q: Some doubted your ability to score goals in the Premier League. Did you want to prove them wrong?

A: Not really. I think that even though I scored 17 goals in the season, there will still be people who doubt me in the future. It's always the way, but I've always had the self-belief that I can score goals.

Q: Marcelo Bielsa has played a big role in recent years, what's he like to work under?

A: The best way to explain it is that you literally learn something new every single day from him - he's like a teacher. He's always adding that extra bit of detail to your game, looking for improvements, so that's the biggest thing. Under him I believe there is no limit to how much I can improve because of what he can offer me as a manager. I really appreciate everything he's done for me so far and I think all the boys do. He's been brilliant and there is no limit to what we can learn under him.

Q: Do you see your 2020/21 season goal mark as a target for 2021/22?

A: Ideally, I'd hit 20 goals and 10 assists and still give everything to the team. But I've got to make sure my game isn't just about goals as I have to be doing what the manager needs from me for the team. While I've set that bar there, I've got to try and do better year on year. The natural progression is scoring more, assisting more and being more consistent in terms of what the manager wants.

Q: Did you feel Bielsa was special from the first day you joined the club?

A: As soon as I started working with him, I realised I'd never worked with another manager who is even remotely similar. Everything is unique - the way we train, it's all measured out to perfection, everything is done to within the nearest centimetre. It is hard to explain what we do without actually coming in and watching us train for a week. You'd really have to see the amount of detail which goes into training to believe it.

Q: Leeds always play at a high-intensity so can you explain how hard training sessions are to reach those fitness levels?

A: The sessions generally are full of lots of sprints. Some of them are very long but you might not even think some are that hard, you're not blowing. But when you do the drills, it is literally sprint, stop, sprint. It's all about being able to change the speed quickly. The hard session is the 'murderball' which has become kind of famous. That is harder than a real game and it's only for around 25 minutes. It's probably why we're so fit.

Q: Can Leeds continue to progress in the Premier League?

A: The important thing was staying in the league first time around. Now we've done that, the second year will be even harder this time - we saw that with Sheffield United. Performing well doesn't give you a right to stay in the league next time, so we've got to maintain our position. Once we've had two or three years as a Premier League team, then we can start building up and pushing for Europe. We already try and win every game so, because of the way we play, it wouldn't surprise me if we did come higher up in the table.

Q: Your first and only Premier League goal before Leeds was with Middlesbrough four years ago, so was there ever a time where you thought that might not come again?

A: I never thought that my first Premier League goal was going to come in the first place. I'd had a lot of loans, I'd only started two games at Norwich and I was thinking that I was never going to get a chance to score. I then went to Middlesbrough and although we were relegated and losing at the time (vs Southampton), I think I celebrated my goal. That goal had been such a long time coming for me and it was a big weight off my shoulders. Since then, I've always believed I could play at that level and it was just about getting back there. Time has gone quickly since and now I'm back there.

Q: What was it like to have six loan spells over just five years?

A: Every loan served its own individual purpose. In an ideal world I'd go on loan and play every game and develop as a player, but it didn't always work out like that. Some teams I went on loan to I played every game and learnt a lot as a football player. Others I didn't but instead learnt a lot about myself as a human. They all helped me, whether it was with football or getting tougher mentally by understanding what I had to do in order to get to that level. After time they did get a little bit boring so I'm now glad I've found a home.

Q: You have had injury setbacks on your road to the top. Do you enjoy the challenge of tackling those and coming back stronger?

A: I am a strong believer that everything happens for a reason. The big thing for me when I injured my knees was setting targets and keeping to those. It's the same as when I'm not injured, I'm always setting little targets to try and improve myself as a player every single day.

Q: What's the atmosphere like playing in front of a packed Elland Road?

A: When we were playing West Brom (2019), Pablo Hernandez scored after 10 seconds and we ended up winning the game 4-1. I remember about 15 minutes into the game I was full-on screaming at Tyler Robers and he just couldn't hear me. That wasn't even after we'd scored a goal, that was just the crowd being so up for it. It can be deafening and is a great atmosphere to play in.

Q: Are there any players or individuals that you look up to or seek advice from?

A: I used to work with Ian Wright at MK Dons and I've stayed good friends with him. Fernando Torres was going through a rough patch when I was with him at Chelsea but he was also really great to talk to. Someone who I really respect and give myself a little kick up the butt to is Jamie Vardy. He came into the Premier League late and has scored 100 goals so he's a big inspiration. With what he has achieved, he's put himself up there with the greatest strikers ever in the Premier League.

QUICK-FIRE

Favourite away ground? Villa Park
Pre-match playlist artist? Dave
Favourite instrument to play? Guitar
Favourite sport other than football? Golf
Funniest teammate? Luke Ayling

MILESTONE MOMENTS

Footballers are remembered for setting individual records or winning team trophies. Here we have a list of players and milestone moments. Can you match the superstar to the correct one?

A
PATRICK BAMFORD

B
HARRY KANE

C
JOE WILLOCK

D
YOURI TIELEMANS

E
SADIO MANE

F
SEAMUS COLEMAN

G
SERGIO AGUERO

H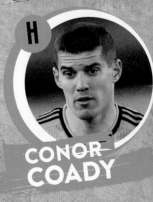
CONOR COADY

1 " I SCORED THE FASTEST PREMIER LEAGUE HAT-TRICK IN JUST 2 MINS 56 SECS IN 2015. "

2 " I WON MY THIRD PREMIER LEAGUE GOLDEN BOOT IN THE 2020/21 SEASON. "

3 " I SCORED A LONG-RANGE SCREAMER TO WIN MY TEAM THE FA CUP IN 2021. "

4 " I AM THE YOUNGEST PLAYER IN PREMIER LEAGUE HISTORY TO SCORE IN SEVEN CONSECUTIVE MATCHES. "

5 " I SCORED MY 184TH PREMIER LEAGUE GOAL ON MY 275TH APPEARANCE. "

6 " I SCORED MY FIRST GOAL FOR MY COUNTRY IN THE 2020/21 SEASON. "

7 " I SCORED MY FIRST PREMIER LEAGUE HAT-TRICK IN 2020. "

8 " I PLAYED MY 300TH PREMIER LEAGUE GAME IN THE 2021/22 SEASON. "

1	2	3	4	5	6	7	8

Answers on page 76

THE AGE GAME

A
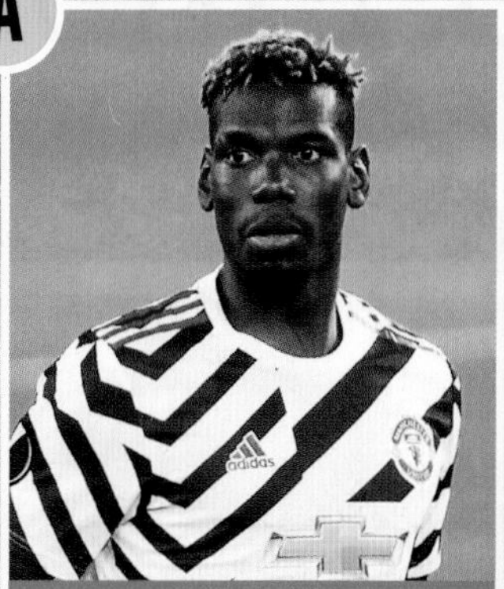
PAUL POGBA

B
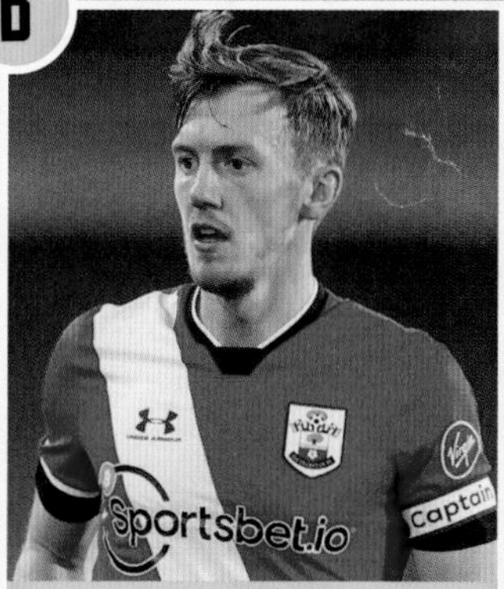

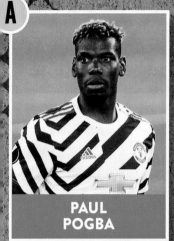

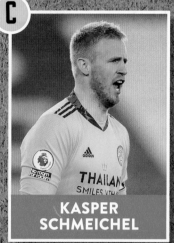

JAMES WARD-PROWSE

C
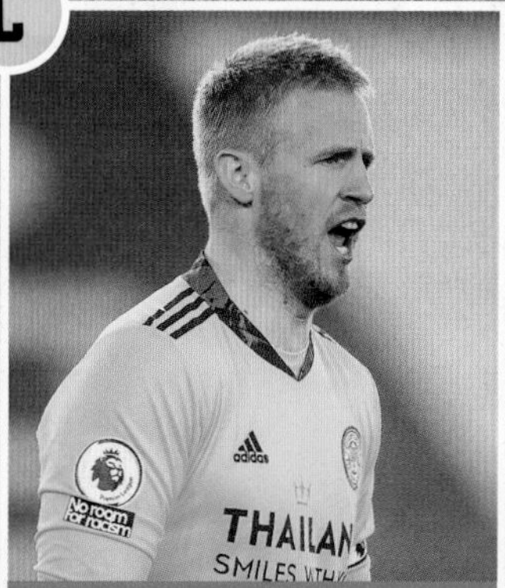
KASPER SCHMEICHEL

D
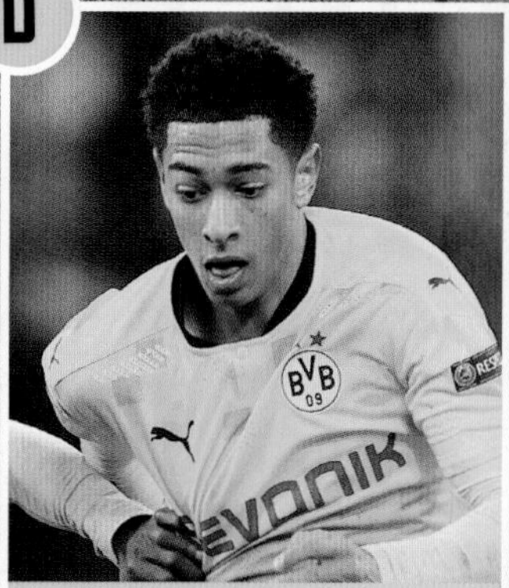
JUDE BELLINGHAM

E
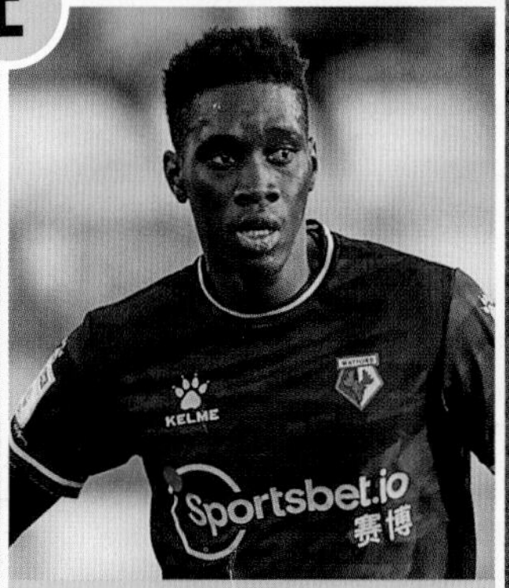

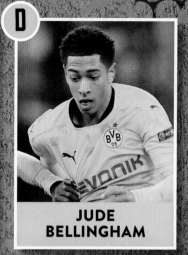

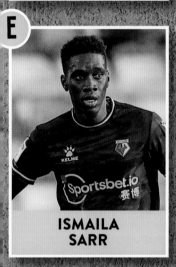

ISMAILA SARR

F
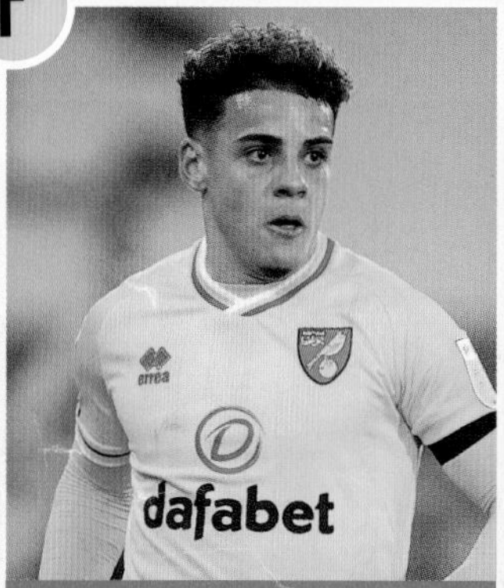

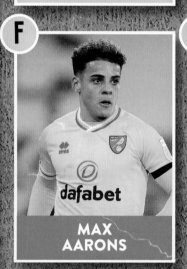

MAX AARONS

G
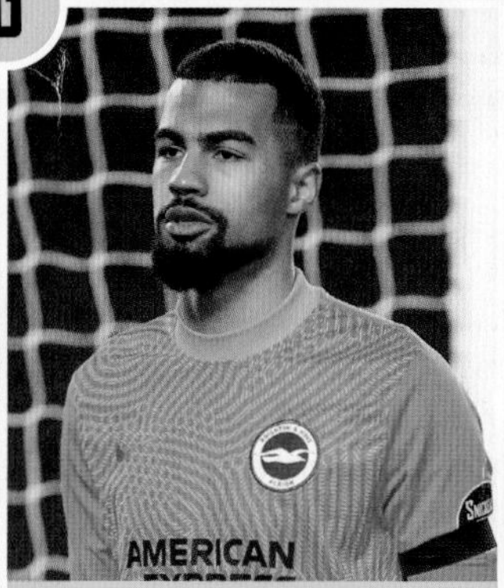

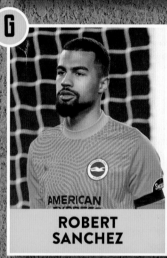

ROBERT SANCHEZ

H
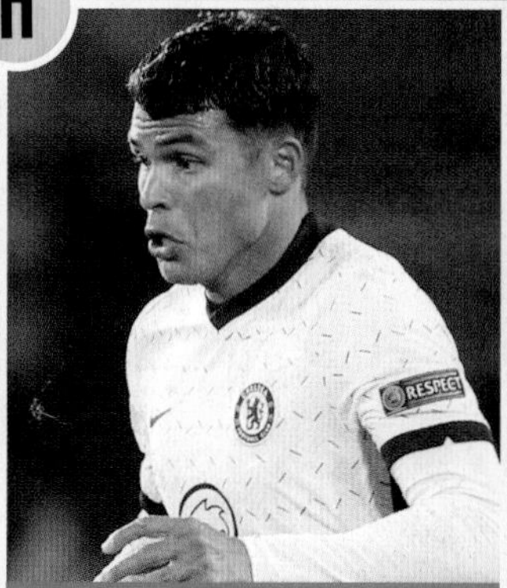

THIAGO SILVA

It is bad manners to ask someone's age but don't worry because these stars won't find out that you are guessing how old they are. So have a go at matching the player to the year you think they were born.

BORN IN **1986** ______

BORN IN **1997** ______

BORN IN **1994** ______

BORN IN **1993** ______

BORN IN **1998** ______

BORN IN **1984** ______

BORN IN **2003** ______

BORN IN **2000** ______

Answers on page 76

SHOOT'S SUPER SQUAD

With so much top talent around we all have an opinion on who are the best footballers in the world. Here at Shoot HQ we have had a go at cutting a huge shortlist down to just 23!

This is what we have come up with. Meet Shoot's Super Squad...

GOALKEEPERS

DOB: 17.08.1993
National Team: Brazil
Star Rating: 4.5

The Brazilian is not only one of the best shot stoppers around but possibly the greatest with the ball at his feet. He can pick out a teammate anywhere on the field with one swing of his boot.

EDERSON

STAR STAT!
Oblak has won the La Liga Best Goalkeeper Award five times!

DOB: 07.01.1993
National Team: Slovenia
Star Rating: 5

Simply one of the most reliable goalkeepers on the planet. Oblak is a real presence between the sticks and is always in control of the defence in front of him.

JAN OBLAK

DOB: 15.12.1986
National Team: Costa Rica
Star Rating: 4

Costa Rican 'keeper Navas has had a career right at the top of the game. His combination of speed, agility and pinpoint distribution means he's still one of the best around.

KEYLOR NAVAS

CENTRE-BACKS

DOB: 08.07.1991
National Team: Netherlands
Star Rating: 5

VVD simply has everything you could ever want a centre-back to have. Quick, strong, good in the air, comfortable with the ball at his feet and almost impossible to beat - that is why he is one of the best there has ever been.

VIRGIL VAN DIJK

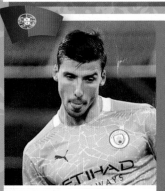

DOB: 14.05.1997
National Team: Portugal
Star Rating: 4.5

The classy Portuguese player has a brilliant all-round game. Dias is a fantastic leader who loves a duel but also bringing the ball out from the back. He could improve any team in the world.

RUBEN DIAS

DOB: 20.06.1991
National Team: Senegal
Star Rating: 4.5

Kalidou Koulibaly adds a string of physical attributes and real pace to the heart of defence. What makes the Senegalese great is his superb positioning, composure on the ball and aerial prowess.

KALIDOU KOULIBALY

DOB: 25.04.1993
National Team: France
Star Rating: 4.5

Serial Champions League winner Raphael Varane is blessed with lightning-quick speed and a tall, strong frame. The Frenchman is also composed on the ball which really makes him the full package.

RAPHAEL VARANE

STAR STAT!
Davies became the first Canadian player to win the men's Champions League in August 2020.

FULL-BACKS

DOB: 02.11.2000
National Team: Canada
Star Rating: 4.5

Alphonso Davies transitioned from a promising left-winger to world class left-back but he has not lost any of his attacking flair. The Canadian uses his dynamic pace to easily cover both ends of the pitch.

ALPHONSO DAVIES

DOB: 12.07.1995
National Team: England
Star Rating: 4

Luke Shaw brings a mature and composed style to the left hand side. The Englishman loves to use his power to drive down the flank but is also more than capable of defending any winger.

LUKE SHAW

DOB: 27.05.1994
National Team: Portugal
Star Rating: 4

Joao Cancelo is an attacking and versatile wing-back who can fit any position on either wing. The Portuguese is also blessed with pace, tight dribbling and exceptional passing. A fantastic option in any squad.

JOAO CANCELO

DOB: 07.10.1998
National Team: England
Star Rating: 4.5

Trent Alexander-Arnold is known for his attacking prowess and pinpoint passing. There is no other player better than the Englishman when it comes to feeding forwards from the right hand side of the pitch.

TRENT ALEXANDER-ARNOLD

STAR STAT!
Ajax paid Willem II just €1 to sign De Jong in 2015.

MIDFIELDERS

DOB: 29.03.1991
National Team: France
Star Rating: 4.5

N'Golo Kante is a player who doesn't stop running in the middle of the park. The Frenchman is the best around at breaking up play but can also use the ball in a more advanced role if needed.

N'GOLO KANTE

DOB: 12.05.1997
National Team: Netherlands
Star Rating: 4

Frenkie de Jong is a fluid playmaker with twinkle toes and robust defensive skills. The Dutchman can steal the ball and carve open any opposition defence with one pass in the blink of an eye.

FRENKIE DE JONG

DOB: 08.09.1994
National Team: Portugal
Star Rating: 4.5

Bruno Fernandes is ice-cool with the ball but filled with passion, flair and a natural will to win. The Portuguese's sharp shooting and wicked deliveries make him the perfect playmaker.

BRUNO FERNANDES

DOB: 28.06.1991
National Team: Belgium
Star Rating: 5

Kevin De Bruyne can unlock any opponent in a flash with a defence-splitting pass. The brilliant Belgian has two strong feet, can drive with the ball, shoot from range and isn't shy when it comes to making a tackle.

KEVIN DE BRUYNE

FORWARDS

STAR STAT!
Ronaldo has won five Ballon d'Or awards (just one behind Messi).

SON HEUNG-MIN

DOB: 08.07.1992
National Team: South Korea
Star Rating: 4.5

Son Heung-min always delivers regular goals and assists and seems to improve season after season. The speedy South Korean can play almost anywhere across an attack and is one of the best dribblers around.

CRISTIANO RONALDO

DOB: 05.02.1985
National Team: Portugal
Star Rating: 5

Quick, powerful, great in the air and with the ball at his feet, Cristiano Ronaldo has been at the top of the game for over a decade. The Portuguese goal machine continues to break record after record and win trophy after trophy.

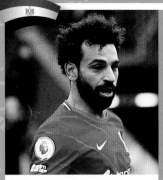

MOHAMAD SALAH

DOB: 15.06.1992
National Team: Egypt
Star Rating: 4.5

Mohamad Salah has a wand of a left foot and always a trick up his sleeve. The Egyptian has proven himself to be one of the sharpest forwards on the planet and has scored a bucket load of goals in recent seasons.

NEYMAR

DOB: 05.02.1992
National Team: Brazil
Star Rating: 4.5

Neymar has made a name for himself with delightful tricks and delicate turns but is far more than just a show-boater. The Brazilian pairs skill with an end product which means any match he features in will be an exciting watch.

STAR STAT!
Mbappe and Brazilian legend Pele are the only two teenagers to have scored in a World Cup final.

STRIKERS

KYLIAN MBAPPE

DOB: 20.12.1998
National Team: France
Star Rating: 5

Kylian Mbappe loves to put on a show on the biggest stages in world football. The Frenchman's lightning quick movements put him more than one step ahead of defenders at all times. Blink and you will miss him.

ROBERT LEWANDOWSKI

DOB: 21.08.1988
National Team: Poland
Star Rating: 5

Robert Lewandowski has been netting goals at the top level for over a decade and seems to get better with age. The prolific Pole has his clinical finishing and impossible-to-mark positioning to thank for an insane record.

ERLING HAALAND

DOB: 21.07.2000
National Team: Norway
Star Rating: 4.5

Erling Haaland has propelled himself into the spotlight with blistering pace, ox-like strength, laser-beam shooting and a real thirst for goals, goals and more goals. The Norwegian has the world at his feet.

HARRY KANE

DOB: 28.07.1993
National Team: England
Star Rating: 5

Harry Kane is a natural goalscorer, leader and a 'proper' number nine. The England skipper is industrious, inventive and has a habit of finding the back of the net with both feet or his head.

SUPER XI

Ever wondered what it is like to be a top football manager? Well now is your chance to show you have what it takes to stand in the dugout. You will need to make tough decisions to become a top manager.

10

STRIKER

9

STRIKER

11

FORWARD

7

FORWARD

6

MIDFIELDER

8

MIDFIELDER

3

FULL-BACK

2

FULL-BACK

4

CENTRE-BACK

5

CENTRE-BACK

1

GOALKEEPER

Start your journey by picking your starting XI from Shoot's Super Squad. Be prepared to deal with some unhappy superstars you leave on the bench.

TEAM NAME:

MANAGER'S NAME:

2021 RECORDS

Records are smashed every single year in the world of football. Here are some standout achievements set in 2021...

Cristiano Ronaldo became the first player to play at five Euros and the tournament's all-time leading goalscorer. He will be 39 when the next one is played.

Celtic and Juventus missed out but Ludogorets won a 10th Bulgarian league title in a row. They had not even played in the top-flight before starting this winning streak.

Kevin Ellison, aged 42, became the oldest player to score in EFL play-off history. A true golden oldie.

Ivan Toney broke the record for most Championship goals in a single season (31). Derby County scored just 36 in the whole season.

Robert Lewandowski scored 41 Bundesliga goals to break Gerd Muller's 49-year-old record. That still wasn't enough for him to win the Player of the Year award.

Newport County goalkeeper Tom King scored the longest goal in a competitive match against Cheltenham Town (96.01m). Now that's long-ball football.

Salford City became the shortest holders of the EFL Trophy (one day) after beating the longest ever holders, Portsmouth (two years). We're sure they still had a fun 24 hours.

Erling Haaland became the fastest player to reach 20 Champions League goals (in just 14 matches). Almost as fast as he sprints!

Manchester City were the lowest placed team at Christmas (8th) to ever win a Premier League title. What did Pep feed them for Christmas lunch?

Blackpool's Oliver Turton scored the fastest own goal (48 seconds) at Wembley Stadium in club football history. Luckily his side came from behind to win!

Marine vs Tottenham in the FA Cup third round was the biggest mismatch in English cup history, with 161 places separating them. No real shock that Spurs won 5-0.

Thiago is the son of Brazilian 1994 World Cup winner Mazinho and his brother is current Paris Saint-Germain midfielder Rafinha.

STAR STAT!
Thiago was actually eligible to play for three of the biggest countries in the footballing world - Spain, Brazil and Italy.

DOB:
11.04.1991 - SAN PIETRO VERNOTICO, ITALY

ALL YOU NEED TO KNOW ABOUT...
THIAGO

3 FAMOUS MANAGERS:

CARLO ANCELOTTI (Bayern Munich)
PEP GUARDIOLA (Barcelona, Bayern Munich)
JURGEN KLOPP (Liverpool)

QUIZ QUESTION:

Which sport did Thiago's Brazilian mother compete in?

A: Tennis
B: MMA
C: Volleyball

....

Answer on page 76

3 FAMOUS TEAMMATES:

OBERT LEWANDOWSKI (Bayern Munich)
LIONEL MESSI (Barcelona)
MOHAMED SALAH (Liverpool)

FACT FILE

INTERNATIONAL:

TEAM: Spain
DEBUT: vs Italy (10 August 2011)
FIRST GOAL: vs Albania (6 October 2017)

TRANSFER FEES:

JULY 2013 – Barcelona to Bayern Munich – £21.5m
SEPTEMBER 2020 — Bayern Munich to Liverpool – £25m
COMBINED TRANSFER FEE: £46.5m

TROPHIES:

CLUB: Champions League x 2, La Liga x 4, Bundesliga x 7, Copa Del Rey, DFB Pokal x 4, Spanish Super Cup x 2, German Super Cup x 3, FIFA Club World Cup x 2, UEFA Super Cup,

COUNTRY: UEFA European Under-21 Championship x 2, UEFA European Under-17 Championship.

SENIOR CAREER TIMELINE:

Barcelona B
2008-2011

Barcelona
2009-2013

Bayern Munich
2013-2020

Liverpool
2020-present

25

SPOT THE STARS!

Eight footballing superstars have decided to go and watch a match on their day off. Can you pick their faces out in the crowd?

26

ON HEUNG-MIN

EMILE SMITH ROWE

JOHN MCGINN

SAID BENRAHMA

FABINHO

HARRY MAGUIRE

RAHEEM STERLING

KELECHI IHEANACHO

Answers on page 76

Euro 2020 Recap

IT'S COMING H~~OM~~E ROME

Euro 2020 took place a year later than planned but it was a tournament well worth waiting for.

Kicking off with Italy against Turkey in Rome, 51 matches were played over 31 days in 11 cities across Europe to celebrate the competition's 60th birthday.

England gave their fans a summer to remember by beating Germany on their way to reaching a first major tournament final since 1966.

Gareth Southgate's men came so close to ending 55 years of hurt but were defeated by Italy on penalties at Wembley Stadium in a heartbreaking end to a magical month.

The Azzurri were deserved winners of their first European Championship since 1968 as Roberto Mancini's side stretched their unbeaten run to 34 matches by the end of the competition.

The other home nations also had a lot to be proud of with Scotland securing a 0-0 draw against England at Wembley in their first major tournament since 1998.

Meanwhile, Wales reached the knockout stage before being eliminated by an inspired Denmark, who were without their talisman Christian Eriksen after he suffered a frightening cardiac arrest in the opening game.

Favourites France, Belgium, and defending champions Portugal, all failed to live up to expectations but Czech Republic, Switzerland and Ukraine all caused surprises.

With 2.78 goals per match, superstar performances from the big names and new stars creating the headlines, Euro 2020 was one of the most exciting international tournaments there has ever been.

Now it's time to relive your Euro memories as we take a look back at the biggest football event of 2021...

Massimo Insabato/Mondadori Portfolio via ZUMA/Shutterstock

VENUES:

Wembley Stadium
London (England)
Capacity: 90,000
Matches: 8

Stadio Olimpico
Rome (Italy)
Capacity: 73,000
Matches: 4

Allianz Arena
Munich (Germany)
Capacity: 75,000
Matches: 4

Baku Olympic Stadium
Baku (Azerbaijan)
Capacity: 65,000
Matches: 4

Gazprom Arena
Saint Petersburg
(Russia)
Capacity: 56,000
Matches: 7

Puskas Arena
Budapest (Hungary)
Capacity: 68,000
Matches: 4

GROUP STAGE:

GROUP A:

Italy showed why they had gone unbeaten since 2018 as they cruised through in top spot with three wins from their three games. Wales, inspired by Gareth Bale and Aaron Ramsey, qualified in second with four points. Switzerland also progressed after finishing behind the Welsh on goal difference but Turkey made an early exit after losing all three of their games.

GROUP B:

Belgium won all three of their games to finish top. Denmark lost their first two games and star man Christian Eriksen after he suffered a cardiac arrest against Finland. The midfielder thankfully recovered in hospital and the Danes ended up qualifying in second after a 4-1 win over Russia in their last game. Finland and Russia packed their bags and headed home.

GROUP C:

Netherlands joined the group of teams to go through with a 100% record in the group stage. The Dutch entertained as they scored eight goals in their three matches. Austria were not far behind in second after winning two of their three games. Ukraine also qualified with just one win in third but debutants North Macedonia were knocked out with no points to show.

GROUP D:

Raheem Sterling scored two winners for England either side of a 0-0 draw against Scotland as a solid Three Lions side finished top. That was the Scots' only point on their return to tournament football as they exited after losing to Croatia, who qualified in second. Czech Republic also went through in third thanks to three goals from striker Patrik Schick.

GROUP E:

Sweden finished top after following up a 0-0 draw against Spain with victories against Slovakia and Poland. The Spaniards, who won the tournament in 1964, 2008 and 2012, claimed second place after eliminating Slovakia with a 5-0 thrashing in the final game. Poland were also knocked out of the competition despite superstar striker Robert Lewandowski netting three goals in the three group games.

GROUP F:

World Cup holders France finished top of the table labelled the 'Group of Death' after a win over Germany was followed with draws against Portugal and Hungary. Germany were six minutes from going out until Leon Goretzka's goal saw them secure a draw against Hungary which pushed them up into second place. That saw defending champions Portugal qualify in third mainly thanks to five group stage goals from serial record-breaker Cristiano Ronaldo.

Arena Nationala
Bucharest (Romania)
Capacity: 56,000
Matches: 4

Johan Cruyff
Arena Amsterdam
(Netherlands)
Capacity: 54,000
Matches: 4

Estadio La Cartuja
Sevilla (Spain)
Capacity: 60,000
Matches: 4

Hampden Park
Glasgow (Scotland)
Capacity: 52,000
Matches: 4

Parken
Copenhagen
(Denmark)
Capacity: 38,000
Matches: 4

KNOCKOUT STAGE:

LAST 16

BELGIUM 1-0 PORTUGAL

Ronaldo and the champions were knocked out thanks to Thorgan Hazard's long-range strike.

ITALY 2-1 AUSTRIA (A.E.T.)

Federico Chiesa and Matteo Pessina sealed Italy's progress against the brave Austrians.

FRANCE 3-3 SWITZERLAND
(SWITZERLAND WIN 5-4 ON PENALTIES)

Kylian Mbappe's spot kick was saved by Yann Sommer as Switzerland caused the biggest shock of Euro 2020.

CROATIA 3-5 SPAIN (A.E.T.)

Croatia scored two late goals to rescue a draw but Morata and Oyarzabal secured Spain's progress.

SWEDEN 1-2 UKRAINE (A.E.T.)

Everyone was ready for penalties when Artem Dovbyk headed home a 121st minute winner for Ukraine.

ENGLAND 2-0 GERMANY

Sterling and Kane scored at Wembley to seal England's first knockout win over Germany since 1966.

WALES 0-4 DENMARK

Gareth Bale and his fellow Dragons ran out of fire as they were thrashed by the determined Danes.

NETHERLANDS 0-2 CZECH REPUBLIC

Netherlands were stunned by Czech Republic who struck after Dutch star De Ligt was sent off.

QUARTER-FINALS

BELGIUM 1-2 ITALY

Goals from Nicolo Barella and Lorenzo Insigne knocked out the world's top ranked team.

SWITZERLAND 1-1 SPAIN (A.E.T.)

La Roja edged through 3-1 on penalties after the Swiss missed three of their four spot kicks.

CZECH REPUBLIC 1-2 DENMARK

Czech Republic put up a fight but Denmark's first half double sealed a first semi-final since 1992.

ENGLAND 4-0 UKRAINE

The Three Lions hit four against Ukraine in Rome with captain Harry Kane scoring twice.

SEMI-FINALS

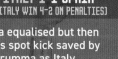

ENGLAND 2-1 DENMARK (A.E.T.)

Kane's extra time goal saw England come from behind to seal a spot in a first major final for 55 years.

ITALY 1-1 SPAIN
(ITALY WIN 4-2 ON PENALTIES)

Morata equalised but then saw his spot kick saved by Donnarumma as Italy reached a fourth Euros final.

FINAL

Andy Rain/AP/Shutterstock

ENGLAND 1-1 ITALY (ITALY WIN 3-2 ON PENALTIES)

Luke Shaw had fans believing that football was coming home when he scored a sweet half volley in just the second minute at Wembley, but Italy fought back through Bonucci's second half goal. Pickford made two great saves in the shootout but Donnarumma became the hero as England missed their last three kicks resulting in the Azzurri lifting the trophy for the first time since 1968.

Maurizio Borsari/AFLO/Shutterstock

UEFA EURO 2020 AWARDS:

Player of the Tournament: **Gianluigi Donnarumma (Italy)**

Young Player: **Pedri (Spain)**

Top Scorer: **Cristiano Ronaldo (Portugal) – 5 goals**

Team of the Tournament: **Gianluigi Donnarumma (Italy);
Kyle Walker (England), Leonardo Bonucci (Italy),
Harry Maguire (England), Leonardo Spinazzola (Italy);
Jorginho (Italy), Pierre-Emile Hojbjerg (Denmark),
Pedri (Spain); Federico Chiesa (Italy),
Romelu Lukaku (Belgium),
Raheem Sterling (England)**

Sterling was a nightmare for opposing defenders throughout the tournament. The forward scored the Three Lions' only two goals of the group stage, netted in the iconic victory over Germany and won THE penalty in the triumphant semi-final against Denmark. Outstanding!

EUROS IN NUMBERS:

1 – North Macedonia and Finland played in their first Euros.

5 – England goalkeeper Jordan Pickford kept a tournament high five clean sheets.

8 – There were eight penalties scored and eight missed (excluding shootouts).

13 – Italy and Spain scored a leading 13 goals at the tournament.

17 – Poland's Kacper Kozłowski was the tournament's youngest player at 17 years and and 246 days.

21 – Switzerland goalkeeper Yann Sommer made a tournament high 21 saves.

38 – Netherlands goalkeeper Maarten Stekelenburg was the tournament's oldest player at 38 years and 278 days.

82 - Emil Forsberg's goal after 82 seconds for Sweden vs Poland was the second-fastest in Euros history.

142 - A Euros record 142 goals were scored at the tournament.

149 – Referees gave out 149 cards (143 yellows and 6 reds) in the tournament.

800 - Haris Seferovic's first goal for Switzerland vs France was the 800th scored in Euros history.

1,099,278 – Nearly 1.1 million fans attended the 51 matches.

FIRST CLUB

Match these stars to the club where they started their rise to the top.

Answers on page 76

GARETH BALE

CHRIS SMALLING

PIERRE-EMERICK AUBAMEYANG

SCORE:

.... /6

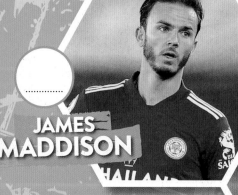

JAMES MADDISON

SADIO MANE

AYMERIC LAPORTE

A AC Milan

F Coventry City

B Basconia

C Maidstone United

D Southampton

E FC Metz

LAST CLUB

Match these legends to the club where they ended their playing days.

B Feyenoord

C New York City FC

D West Ham United

E Qingdao Huanghai FC

A New York Red Bulls

PATRICE EVRA

PETER CROUCH

F Burnley

ROBERT VAN PERSIE

SCORE:

.... /6

FRANK LAMPARD

YAYA TOURE

THIERRY HENRY

Answers on page 76

WATFORD

Ben Foster has launched himself into becoming YouTube's most popular goalkeeper armed with just a small collection of video cameras and a bicycle. The shot stopper's hilarious, access-all-areas insight into life as a professional footballer has gained over half a million subscribers! We sat down with Ben to find out more about The Cycling GK and a career between the sticks.

THE CYCLING GK

BEN FOSTER
THE CYCLING GK

The footballer with over half a million YouTube subscribers!

Q: What made you start the channel?

A: We were literally running out of things to do and to keep the kids busy in the very first lockdown (March 2020). We were doing so much random stuff in the garden like football challenges, netball challenges, assault courses, setting up slipping slides, spray painting grids on the grass, and I thought it'd be pretty cool if I could show this to other people on YouTube. The idea was to make them aware that if I could do that in my garden, they could possibly do the same. Then we were playing against Luton and I just stuck the camera in the back of my goal just to see what would happen. We put that video out on YouTube and the reaction to it straight away was just incredible. People never get to see a game from that angle, they never get to be that close to it. That was when we realised we might be onto something.

Q: Is cycling something you've found later in your career?

A: I've been doing it for a long time and have probably been out on the road for about 10 years now. I've had so many injuries through playing and, because I'm a big guy, I can't really run. Running is not an option for me as my knees will just get sore so I found that cycling is just the best way to be able to keep my fitness levels up. It's a real stress reliever and it also means I can still have a guilt-free burger and some chips at the end of the day.

Q: Did you ever think that The Cycling GK would be as popular as it is?

A: Honestly, no. I always used YouTube to watch a lot of cycling but I'm very much new to it and I didn't honestly understand how big of a world it is. I think the reason people love it so much is people had never really seen what it's like to be a footballer. They see what a club or league will put out but that is always watered down to an extent because they can only show so much. Whereas I'm at a stage in my career where I have done so much already that I'm happy to share things you wouldn't see anywhere else.

Q: Do you find it gives you a nice mental break from the pressures of football?

A: For sure. There is so much stress and pressure involved in football that I just find that whenever I go out on my bike, I just feel good to get back to it after. Cycling is perfect for me because I can go early in the day and the rest of the day is still mine.

Q: How have your teammates reacted?

A: I remember bringing the camera out and the lads were a bit sceptical at first. They wondered why I was pulling the camera out here, there and everywhere? Then once they started seeing what the content actually was and the story it told, they all got on board and now really enjoy it. They all don't mind jumping in front of the camera and doing bits and bobs.

Q: What was it like to bounce back to the Premier League at the first attempt with Watford?

A: To get out of the Championship it is such a hard league. It started really well for us but it's relentless, you have games every three or four days without fail. We really struggled in the early part to keep stringing wins together. We then got battered but got away with a 0-0 draw at Coventry and we could all sense that something wasn't right. We had a big old team meeting where we put the world to rights and regrouped. In the next match we beat Bristol City 6-0 and we never really looked back. We put an incredible run together at the right time to shoot up the league and seal promotion with two games to go.

Q: Are you enjoying your football now more than and ever?

A: I'm definitely enjoying it more. Once you get a bit older you realise you should be enjoying yourself. I have literally got the dream job so I should go out and enjoy every game, with a smile on my face. I'm now doing it the way I do in training, where we're all just smiling and having a good time. It's not always easy to do when it comes to a game but I've now learnt how to manage that situation better.

Q: What advice would you give any young goalkeeper?

A: The biggest thing I will always say to kids is to just try and be comfortable in what you are and who you are. If you can be comfortable in your own skin, then you can absolutely smash anything you want to do. Know your limitations, know your capabilities and go out and play with a smile on your face.

Q: What does the future look like for The Cycling GK channel?

A: The big thing for the channel was getting promoted back to the Premier League. I can now do all the GoPro and matchday vlogs but at the big away stadiums like Man City, Man United and Liverpool. People have got a buzz off seeing the content but taking it to the Premier League is just next level. We've also got some great collaborations lined up with some huge YouTube names and hopefully many more things to come on top of that. Basically the aim is to just move it on to bigger and better things.

FACT FILE

NAME: BEN FOSTER
DOB: 3.04.1983 – LEAMINGTON SPA, ENGLAND
POSITION: GOALKEEPER
CLUB: WATFORD
INTERNATIONAL: ENGLAND (8 CAPS)

QUICK-FIRE

Q: Favourite food after a long ride?

A: Burger. That's my go-to cheap meal if ever I can treat myself.

Q: Longest you have ridden in one go?

A: 100 miles in RideLondon. It was a wicked atmosphere and such good fun.

Q: Greatest footballing achievements

A: My England debut and winning the League Cup with Birmingham against Arsenal in 2011.

Q: Pre-season training session or 100-mile ride?

A: 100-mile ride, all day long!

Q: Favourite professional cyclist

A: Tao Geoghegan Hart

Q: Will you ever give up creating the thumbnails for your YouTube channel?

A: Never, ever, ever!

THE CYCLING GK

CLUB CAREER

There are lots of transfers in the modern game. This means footballers can end up playing for many clubs during their careers. Can you name these six current Premier League stars by looking at the teams they have played for..?

 SC Heerenveen
 Stocksbridge Park Steels
 Oadby Town
 Maine Road FC
 Danubio FC
 Lille

 FC Twente
 Halifax Town
 Ilkeston
 Oldham Athletic
 Palermo
 Paris Saint-Germain

 Ajax
 Fleetwood Town
 Sheffield United
 Brentford
 Napoli
 Roma

 Chelsea
 Leicester City
 Birmingham City
 Burnley
 **Paris Saint-Germain**
 FC Barcelona

 **Southampton**
 **Manchester United**
 **Everton**

Player 1	Player 2	Player 3	Player 4	Player 5	Player 6
....	....	....	....	....	....

Answers on page 77

LEGENDARY LINK-UP

Kalvin Phillips at Leeds United, Mason Mount at Chelsea and Marcus Rashford at Manchester United are three current stars slowly becoming legends at their clubs. But what do you know about legendary players from previous eras?

Link the footballer to the club where they are worshipped by the fans.

Good luck!

LEDLEY KING ☐

DUNCAN FERGUSON ☐

IAN RUSH ☐

BOBBY MOORE ☐

DAVID BECKHAM ☐

LUTHER BLISSETT ☐

DAVID SEAMAN ☐

DIDIER DROGBA ☐

A

B

C

D

E

F

G

H

SCORE /8

Answers on page 77

2021 Winners

WHO'S WON WHAT IN 2021..?

PREMIER LEAGUE:
Man City

FA CUP:
Men's: Leicester City / Women's: ....

LEAGUE CUP:
Men's: **Man City** / Women's: **Chelsea**

CHAMPIONS LEAGUE:
Men's: **Chelsea** / Women's: **Barcelona**

COMMUNITY SHIELD:
Men's: **Man City / Leicester City** (cross out the losing team)
Women's: **Man City / Chelsea** (cross out the losing team)

WSL: Chelsea

WSL CHAMPIONSHIP: Leicester City

EUROPA LEAGUE: Villarreal

UEFA SUPER CUP:
Chelsea / Villarreal (cross out the losing team)

CHAMPIONSHIP:
Winners: **Norwich**, 2nd: **Watford**, Play-Off champs: **Brentford**

LEAGUE ONE:
Winners: **Hull**, 2nd: **Peterborough**, Play-Off champs: **Blackpool**

LEAGUE TWO:
Winners: **Cheltenham**, 2nd: **Cambridge**, 3rd: **Bolton**
Play-Off champs: **Morecambe**

NATIONAL LEAGUE:
Winners: **Sutton**, Play-Off champs: **Hartlepool United**

SCOTLAND:
Scottish Premier League: **Rangers**
Scottish Cup & League Cup: **St Johnstone**
Women's Premier League: **Glasgow City**

EURO LEAGUES:
Spain: **Atletico Madrid** / Italy: **Inter Milan** / France: **Lille**
Germany: **Bayern Munich** / Portugal: **Sporting CP**

EURO 2020 (...IN 2021): **Italy**

OLYMPIC GAMES: Men's: _____
Women's: _____

EFL CHALLENGE

WHICH CLUBS PLAY IN WHICH LEAGUE?

The EFL sees 72 clubs competing across three leagues every season. But with 10 promotion and 9 relegation spots each year, keeping track of which team is in which division is not always easy. Here is your chance to show us your EFL knowledge by matching the clubs below with the league they will play their football in during the 2021/22 season.

TIP: WE HAVE INCLUDED THREE CLUBS FROM EACH LEAGUE TO MAKE YOUR MISSION SLIGHTLY EASIER.

Birmingham City

Accrington Stanley

Bristol Rovers

Sunderland

Huddesfield Town

Oldham Athletic

Millwall

Salford City

Ipswich Town

CHAMPIONSHIP

LEAGUE ONE

LEAGUE TWO

WHO AM I?

Can you use the clues to reveal the identity of these footballers..?

CLUE 1:
A forward who loves to dribble with the ball.

CLUE 2:
Moved from the Hoops to the Eagles in 2020.

CLUE 3:
Scored a wonder goal vs Sheffield United in his first Premier League season.

....
....

CLUE 1:
Loves to pick a pass and make a tackle in the middle of the park.

CLUE 2:
Plays for his hometown club.

CLUE 3:
Made his Premier League and England debuts in 2020.

....
....

CLUE 1:
Can play as a defensive midfielder or a centre-back.

CLUE 2:
Played one game for Real Madrid in 2013.

CLUE 3:
Has won league titles in France and England.

....
....

CLUE 1:
Captained both club and country.

CLUE 2:
Scored at the 2018 World Cup and Euro 2020.

CLUE 3:
Became the world's most expensive defender in 2019.

....
....

Answers on page 77

QUIZ OF THE YEAR

A lot has happened in the world of football in 2021, but how much do you remember? Put your knowledge to the test and build as many points as possible by taking on our Quiz of the Year. The questions get harder as you move on so we will reward you by offering more points if you get them right.

EXAMPLE...
Correct answer for question 1 = 1 point
Correct answer for question 7 = 7 points
Correct answer for question 15 = 15 points

Add your points together at the end to see how many you scored out of a possible 120.

1 Which player scored both of England's group goals in the Euros? _____

2 In which country did the Olympic Games football tournament take place? _____

3 Chelsea beat Man City in the Champions League final 1-0 but who scored the goal? _____

4 Which former Premier League striker was Inter Milan's top scorer as they won their first Serie A title since 2010? _____

5 Scotland scored their only goal at the Euros against which country? _____

6 Harry Kane won his _____ Premier League Golden Boot?

POINTS BUILDER

7 Former Arsenal manager Unai Emery won his fourth European trophy as a manager but with which club? _____

8 Who topped Wales' group at the Euros after beating the Dragons in the third match? _____

9 Who started their job as England women's head coach in September? _____

10 Wayne Rooney managed to save which club from Championship relegation? _____

11 Which club became the 50th different team to play in the Premier League? _____

12 Which Chelsea star finished top scorer in the Women's Super League (WSL)? _____

13 Ashley Young returned to Aston Villa from Inter Milan but in which year did he first sign for the Villans? _____

14 Jude Bellingham became England's third ever youngest player but at which club did he start his career? _____

15 Sutton United were promoted to the Football League for the first time but what is the club's main home kit colour? _____

SCORE /120

Answers on page 77

CHRISTIAN PULISIC

Christian Pulisic is USA's boy wonder. The winger is the youngest American to start a World Cup qualifying campaign, to score a brace for his country and to captain his national team. It is fair to say that the nation's hopes hinge on him.

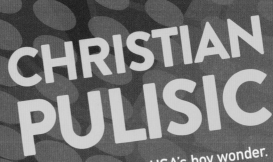

UNITED STATES
DOB: 18.09.1998
POSITION: Winger
NATIONAL TEAM DEBUT:
vs Guatemala (March 2016)

WORLD STARS:

ALL EYES ON QATAR 2022...

Everyone gets football fever in a World Cup year. We are so excited about the next tournament in 2022 that we have picked out some familiar international stars capable of excelling in Qatar... (if their nations qualify).

Javier Garcia/BPI/Shutterstock

EMILIANO MARTINEZ

Emiliano Martinez earned a first cap at the age of 28 after impressing in the Premier League with both Arsenal and Aston Villa. The shot-stopper has already become a penalty saving hero for his country and looks to be the man to have solved a problem position for the South American giants.

ARGENTINA
DOB: 02.09.1992
POSITION: Goalkeeper
NATIONAL TEAM DEBUT:
vs Chile (June 2021)

BRAZIL
DOB: 10.05.1997
POSITION: Forward
NATIONAL TEAM DEBUT:
vs USA (September 2018)

RICHARLISON

Richarlison has already tasted international glory with Brazil after winning the Copa America on home soil in 2019 where he scored the last goal against Peru in the final. The forward is improving season after season and we expect him to continue to influence the national side.

VIRGIL VAN DIJK

Virgil van Dijk is the perfect leader for any team. The powerful centre-back has captained the Netherlands since 2018 and will aim to lead his country to the top of the world… if the Dutch qualify this time after missing out in 2018.

SENEGAL
DOB: 10.04.1992
POSITION: Winger
NATIONAL TEAM DEBUT:
vs Morocco (May 2012)

SADIO MANE

Sadio Mane has been Senegal's talisman for quite some time and is one of his country's leading goalscorers. The attacker netted at the last World Cup in Russia and was key for the Lions of Teranga in their run to the African Cup of Nations final in 2019.

NETHERLANDS
DOB: 08.07.1991
POSITION: Centre-back
NATIONAL TEAM DEBUT: vs Kazakhstan (October 2015)

URUGUAY
DOB: 14.02.1987
POSITION: Striker
NATIONAL TEAM DEBUT:
vs Colombia (February 2008)

EDINSON CAVANI

Edinson Cavani has formed one of international football's best strike partnerships in recent years with Luis Suarez .The classy forward has played over 120 times for his country and has scored over 50 goals. Five of those came at World Cups and Cavani has already stated his desire to play in Qatar.

RIYAD MAHREZ

French-born Riyad Mahrez chose to play for Algeria in 2013. Since then he has captained the Desert Foxes to African Cup of Nations success in 2019 where he scored the winner in the semi-final. He will hope his serial trophy winning habit at club level can continue to rub off on Algeria.

SON HEUNG-MIN

Son Heung-min needs one more World Cup goal to become his country's leading goalscorer in the tournament. The forward has been playing for his country since the age of 18 and has already tasted success on the international stage with gold at the 2018 Asian Games.

ALGERIA
DOB: 21.02.1991
POSITION: Winger
NATIONAL TEAM DEBUT:
vs Armenia (May 2014)

SOUTH KOREA
DOB: 08.07.1992
POSITION: Forward
NATIONAL TEAM DEBUT:
vs Syria (December 2010)

JORGINHO

Jorginho offers creativity and versatility to Italy's midfield. The Brazil-born pass master will be looking to guide a reenergised Azzurri to glory in Qatar after having success in many competitions with Chelsea.

ITALY
DOB: 20.12.1991
POSITION: Midfielder
NATIONAL TEAM DEBUT:
vs Spain (March 2016)

SPAIN
DOB: 11.04.1991
POSITION: Midfielder
NATIONAL TEAM DEBUT:
vs Italy (August 2011)

THIAGO ALCANTARA

Thiago Alcantara was unlucky to miss Spain's successful European Championship campaign in 2012 through injury but has since won a half-century of caps. The midfielder is a highly creative and technical player which could be the key to unlocking La Roja's opponents.

YOURI TIELEMANS

FA Cup hero Youri Tielemans is now living up to all the hype after having been a long-time favourite for football video game fans. The midfielder was first capped by Belgium at the age of 19 but has now developed into a consistent performer capable of running a game at the highest level.

FRANCE
DOB: 29.03.1991
POSITION: Midfielder
NATIONAL TEAM DEBUT: vs Netherlands (March 2016)

N'GOLO KANTE

N'Golo Kante was approached by Mali before he became a France international in 2016. The loveable midfielder has since become a World Cup winner and offers great balance to a Les Bleus side with so much attacking firepower.

BELGIUM
DOB: 07.05.1997
POSITION: Midfielder
NATIONAL TEAM DEBUT: vs Netherlands (November 2016)

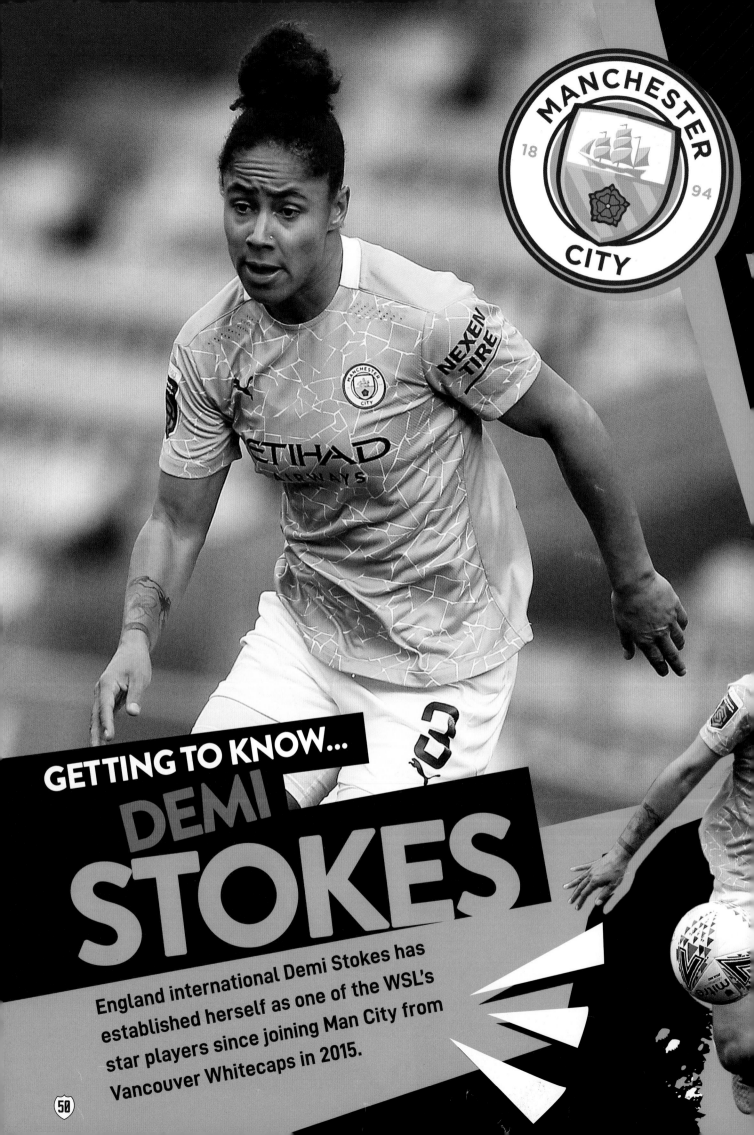

GETTING TO KNOW...
DEMI STOKES

England international Demi Stokes has established herself as one of the WSL's star players since joining Man City from Vancouver Whitecaps in 2015.

MANCHESTER CITY

18 94

ENGLAND AND CITY STAR TAKES ON SHOOT'S QUICK-FIRE ROUND

The dynamic left-back was part of the Lionesses squad which reached the 2019 World Cup semi-final in France and represented Great Britain at the Tokyo Olympics.

At club level, Stokes has won six major trophies to date, including three FA Cups and a first WSL title for Man City in 2016.

Now in her latest challenge, the flying full-back tackles Shoot's quick-fire questions...

CHILDHOOD FOOTBALLING IDOL?
DAVID BECKHAM

FAVOURITE SUMMER ACTIVITY?
BADMINTON – IF IT'S NICE OUT

BEST PLAYER YOU'VE PLAYED AGAINST?
EUGENIE LE SOMMER

FAVOURITE GOAL SCORED?
VS CHELSEA IN 2016

DREAM CONCERT?
BOB MARLEY AND JAY-Z

FUNNIEST TEAMMATE?
JILL SCOTT

FAVOURITE FOOTBALL KIT?
ENGLAND '98 KIT

ONE ITEM YOU'D MOST HATE TO LOSE?
MY NAN'S NECKLACE

ARTIST YOU LISTEN TO PRE-MATCH?
POPCAAN

FAVOURITE PLACE TO HOLIDAY?
VENICE

MOST WATCHED TV SERIES?
POWER

BEST FOOTBALLING MOMENT SO FAR?
WINNING THE FA CUP AT WEMBLEY

DREAM TEAM CAPTAIN?
RONALDINHO

MOST USEFUL TEAMMATE ON A SURVIVAL ISLAND?
LUCY BRONZE

MOST USELESS TEAMMATE ON A SURVIVAL ISLAND?
JILL SCOTT

MORNING OR NIGHT PERSON?
MORNING

SO YOU THINK YOU KNOW...

BUKAYO SAKA?

STAR STAT!
Saka became the youngest England player to start a major tournament semi-final when the Three Lions played Denmark at Euro 2020.

Arsenal

Every football fan has heard of Bukayo Saka. The versatile Arsenal star is already a Premier League regular and took Euro 2020 by storm with his impressive performances. Show us how much you really know about the England international by tackling these true or false questions.

1 Saka signed his first professional deal with Arsenal at the age of 17.
TRUE ☐ FALSE ☐

2 Saka represented Nigeria at youth level.
TRUE ☐ FALSE ☐

3 The word 'Bukayo' originates from Yoruba language, meaning 'adds to happiness'.
TRUE ☐ FALSE ☐

4 Saka achieved four A*s and three As in his GCSEs.
TRUE ☐ FALSE ☐

Answers on page 77

52

5 Saka has never scored a goal for Arsenal.

TRUE ☐ FALSE ☐

6 Saka scored on his England debut against Wales.

TRUE ☐ FALSE ☐

7 Saka played for Arsenal Under-23s as a 17-year-old.

TRUE ☐ FALSE ☐

8 Saka has a brother who played for Watford as a youngster.

TRUE ☐ FALSE ☐

9 Saka won Arsenal's Player of the Year award in 2020/21.

TRUE ☐ FALSE ☐

10 Arsenal's North London rivals Tottenham were Saka's boyhood club.

TRUE ☐ FALSE ☐

HOW DID YOU SCORE?

0-2 You're SAKked!: You need to brush up on your knowledge

3-6 O-kay-o: Not bad at all – good work!

7-10 Saka-bleu!: Top of the class.

Lindsey Parnaby/AP/Shutterstock

53

PREMIER PLAYMAKERS

WHO'S THE BEST PLAYMAKER IN THE LAND?

SHOOT RATES THESE CLASSY CREATORS

KEVIN DE BRUYNE

Kevin De Bruyne is top of the tree when it comes to creative talent. The Belgian won the inaugural Premier League Playmaker award with 16 assists in the 2017/18 season, before winning it again two years later when he set up a record 20 goals.

Playmaker Rating: 5

54

BRUNO FERNANDES

Bruno Fernandes' quality from dead balls and top-notch passing range saw him stack up 19 assists in his first 50 Premier League matches. The Portuguese's frightening vision means he is capable of finding a teammate in the tightest of areas.

Playmaker Rating:
4.5

Playmaker Rating:
3.5

KAI HAVERTZ

After getting off to a slow start, Kai Havertz ended the season showing he has the talent to be a Premier Playmaker... even playing out of position. The German only managed three assists but as time goes on he will tear up defences with his clever movement and passing.

Playmaker Rating:
4

JACK GREALISH

Bucket-loads of flair and positivity are what make Jack Grealish a Premier Playmaker. The England international has some mad skills in the locker and is direct with his dribbling, frightening defenders with every single tricky twist and turn.

RAPHINHA

Ranking in sixth for assists during his debut Premier League season, Raphinha is one of the best when it comes to creating chances. The Brazilian is also a great dribbler of the ball as well... just ask Gary Cahill, who was the victim of an outrageous nutmeg.

Playmaker Rating:
3.5

Arsenal

Jen Beattie's career has taken her around the world to Australia, France and England since leaving her native Scotland as a teenager. The powerful defender has played over 130 times for her country and represented the Tartan Army at two major tournaments. But having tackled one of life's toughest challenges away from the pitch, the Arsenal star is not done yet. Here Jen looks back at her amazing journey, plus reveals that she has her sights firmly set on the 2023 World Cup and taking the Gunners back to the top of the WSL.

Jacques Feeney/SPP/Shutterstock

HARD
TO BEAT!

JOE MONTEMURRO

FACT FILE

NAME: JEN BEATTIE
DOB: 13.05.1991 — GLASGOW, SCOTLAND
POSITION: CENTRE-BACK
CLUBS: QUEEN'S PARK, CELTIC, ARSENAL, MONTPELLIER HSC, MAN CITY, MELBOURNE CITY
INTERNATIONAL: SCOTLAND

Q: How was it to return to Arsenal in 2019 after four years away from the club?

A: It was good. Arsenal had just been crowned champions, so it was a huge step up in that sense. It is always a heavily pressured situation joining the champions. It was obviously great to be back working with Joe Montemurro (ex-Arsenal manager). I worked previously with him in Melbourne, so I jumped at the chance to work with him again.

Q: How different is women's football in England now compared to when you first moved to Arsenal in 2009?

A: Massively different. I was semi-professional when I first joined Arsenal. I was studying business at the University of Hertfordshire, and they gave me a scholarship. So to see it go from semi-pro to a full-time league is amazing. Women's football is on an upwards trajectory where it will just keep growing and growing. The more backing it gets, the bigger it will become.

Q: You spent two years in French football with Montpellier. Did you always plan to play abroad?

A: I always knew I wanted to get out of my comfort zone. Going to Montpellier was the first professional contract that I signed. Arsenal were still semi-pro so it was an opportunity to go full-time and to live in a beautiful part of the world. It was one of the hardest things I have ever done, because I was trying to learn the language and the sessions were all in French. It was tough but also amazing.

Q: What was it like to also play in Australia with Melbourne City?

A: I was really lucky because the link between Manchester City and Melbourne meant I actually got to go and play there on loan during the off-season in England. It was one of the best experiences of my life because Melbourne is an unbelievable city. I got to see the Gold Coast, Perth and we won every single game during my time there. I also had one of my best mates, Kim Little, out there with me too and we lived together. So to experience that with one of my best friends was just incredible.

Q: Can Arsenal close the gap to Man City and Chelsea in the 2021/22 season?

A: It has been so tight up there, which is a credit to the league because it shows how far it has advanced. We got Champions League football but for us, as a club, it wasn't good enough. Most of us want to be lifting trophies so it has been a disappointing two seasons since winning the league. I do think that we can push on and that the gap can be closed this year.

Q: You won numerous trophies with Man City. How did you enjoy your time there and what was the secret behind such a successful team?

A: I absolutely loved my time there and I have nothing but amazing memories of it. Working with Nick Cushing and playing alongside Steph Houghton was an amazing experience. What's the secret? I think it was very intense and it had to be. You don't get away with not working hard, you don't get away with not turning up every day. I think that really pushed me as a player and it was definitely one of the best decisions I ever made to move there. I was 24 at the time and I think it made me realise what it took to be a professional.

Q: You've played over 130 times for Scotland. How much pride do you feel pulling on the shirt?

A: It's a massive sense of pride. We have just come off the back of a relatively successful four or five years by qualifying for two tournaments on the bounce. That's something that I will always be so proud of because it doesn't get much bigger than playing for your country at a major tournament. We were obviously gutted not to get to the Euros (2022), but hopefully we will get to the World Cup. There's nothing better than wearing a Scotland shirt at a major tournament.

Q: What was it like to play and score at the 2019 World Cup after missing Euro 2017 through injury?

A: Qualifying for the Euros was one of the best moments of my career so to miss it through injury was devastating. To then qualify for the following World Cup and make it two tournaments on the bounce for Scotland was great. I actually felt really nervous leading up to the tournament because I was worried that something was going to go wrong again. But to walk out against England in Nice with my parents in the crowd was one of the best moments of my career to date. To then score against Argentina was amazing. It was just a tap in but felt better because of the occasion.

Q: You have played on since being treated for breast cancer in October 2020. What's given you the drive to continue?

A: I think I just wanted normality. I didn't want anything to knock me. I know everybody has had a tough year due to Covid, but for me to not be around family was a hundred times harder than it would normally have been. I just wanted to keep going into training and have that normal feeling of going to work and being around mates and teammates. They were my support system and they were what got me through it. Exercise makes people feel good so I'm very lucky that my job is a very active one.

Q: How supportive have the football community been towards you?

A: The football community was honestly incredible and Arsenal in particular were great. I couldn't have asked for better support and that is something that I am particularly grateful for. I think that's the reason that I got into a team sport. I played a lot of sports when I was younger like tennis, golf and other individual sports. But I have always loved the feeling of being with teammates, meeting different people who all have different characters and different mentalities.

Q: Your dad and brother were former international rugby players so how did you end up playing football?

A: I just never really got into rugby because it wasn't too accessible for girls when I was younger. I can honestly say I have played probably every sport other than rugby. It was Johnny (Jen's brother) and my dad's game but I fell in love with football instead.

Q: You did some broadcasting work during the men's Euros. Is that something that you enjoy and could see yourself going into once you stop playing?

A: It is something so different but something I really enjoyed. You're not on the pitch but it still feels like you're involved somehow. I really enjoyed the aspect of looking at the game differently and getting to work with lots of talented people. I loved learning, the experience of it and would jump at the opportunity if I get offered it again.

Q: What advice would you give to any young footballer?

A: Get the balance right. I think football can be intense and hard work so the number one thing is being able to switch off. You need to be around friends and family and enjoy the other side of life. Be intense when it is intense and work hard when you need to, but you need to find ways to switch off and get away from it. That will stand you in good stead in the long run.

QUICK-FIRE

Favourite city? Melbourne
Favourite goal? vs Argentina (2019 World Cup)
Favourite football kit of all time?
Scotland's 1998 World Cup shirt
Favourite animal? Elephant
Most watched TV boxset?
Friends

1 Chelsea have won the league a record four times.

TRUE ☐ FALSE ☐

3 Reading have the biggest stadium in the 2021/22 season.

TRUE ☐ FALSE ☐

2 10 teams play to win the title each season.

TRUE ☐ FALSE ☐

4 Liverpool are the only side to win the title two seasons in a row.

TRUE ☐ FALSE ☐

5 Arsenal have won more WSL matches than any other club.

TRUE ☐ FALSE ☐

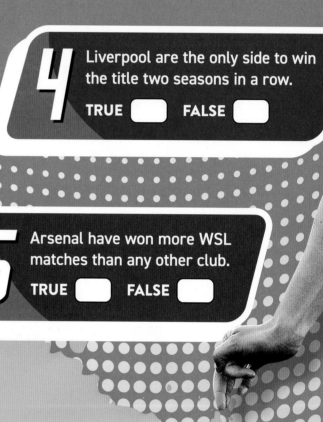

SO YOU THINK YOU KNOW...
THE WSL?

Every football fan knows about the Women's Super League since it kicked off a decade ago! England's top division is also one of the best in the world and has attracted a number of international stars. Show us how much you really know about the WSL by facing these true or false questions?

6 Manchester United won promotion to the WSL in 2016.

TRUE ☐ FALSE ☐

STAR STAT!
Gilly Flaherty, Gemma Davison and Ji So-Yun have each won the WSL a record four times.

7 Birmingham have never been relegated from the WSL.

TRUE ☐ FALSE ☐

8 Ellen White has scored for three different WSL clubs.

TRUE ☐ FALSE ☐

9 Jill Scott has played more WSL matches than any other player.

TRUE ☐ FALSE ☐

10 Lauren James is the youngest ever WSL player.

TRUE ☐ FALSE ☐

HOW DID YOU SCORE?

0-2 Super Fail: Some WSL research is much needed!

3-6 Super Acceptable: Not bad at all – good work!

7-10 Super Smart: You seriously know your WSL!

Craig Galloway/ProSports/Shutterstock

Answers on page 77

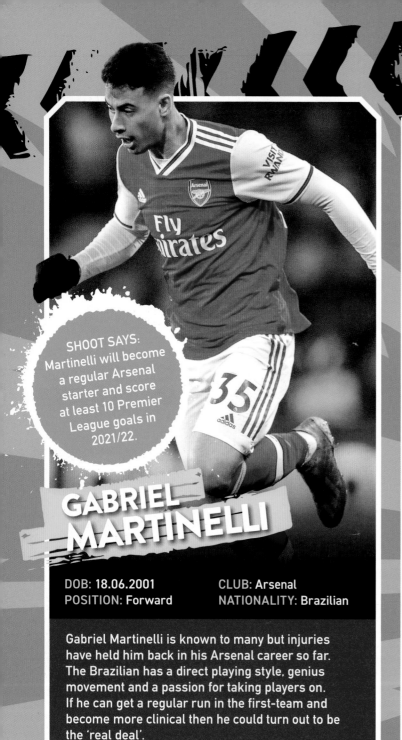

SHOOT SAYS: Martinelli will become a regular Arsenal starter and score at least 10 Premier League goals in 2021/22.

SHOOT SAYS: Elanga to make his senior international debut during the 2021/22 season.

GABRIEL MARTINELLI

DOB: 18.06.2001
POSITION: Forward
CLUB: Arsenal
NATIONALITY: Brazilian

Gabriel Martinelli is known to many but injuries have held him back in his Arsenal career so far. The Brazilian has a direct playing style, genius movement and a passion for taking players on. If he can get a regular run in the first-team and become more clinical then he could turn out to be the 'real deal'.

ANTHONY ELANGA

DOB: 27.04.2002
POSITION: Winger
CLUB: Manchester United
NATIONALITY: Swedish

Anthony Elanga has progressed through the club's academy since joining from Malmo in 2014 and has been prolific in United's youth teams. The winger can score goals from either side of the pitch and has great acceleration. After scoring in just his second Premier League match, fans will be expecting big things from the Swede over the next few seasons.

WONDERKIDS

Every young player has dreams of bossing the Premier League and some manage to do just that season after season. Phil Foden, Mason Greenwood and Bukayo Saka are all recent examples of young stars to light up England's big league. Here we have listed six young guns we think will be next to hit the headlines.

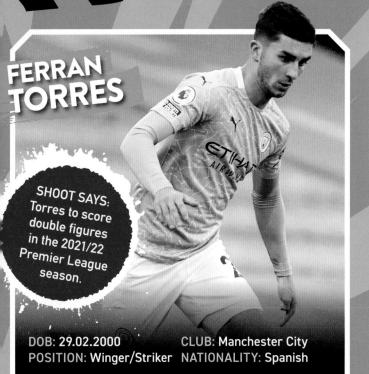

FERRAN TORRES

SHOOT SAYS: Torres to score double figures in the 2021/22 Premier League season.

DOB: 29.02.2000
POSITION: Winger/Striker
CLUB: Manchester City
NATIONALITY: Spanish

Ferran Torres has shown more than flashes of what he is capable of already by scoring hat-tricks for Man City and Spain. The forward's versatility, dribbling and inventive finishing make him one you should definitely watch. He will no doubt improve with age and experience.

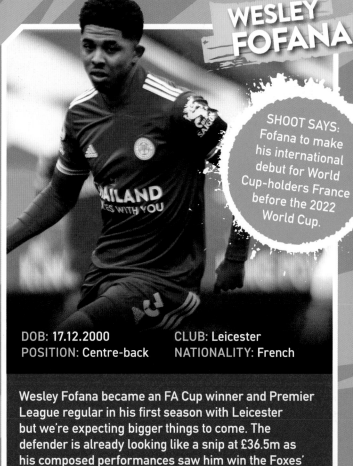

WESLEY FOFANA

SHOOT SAYS: Fofana to make his international debut for World Cup-holders France before the 2022 World Cup.

DOB: 17.12.2000
POSITION: Centre-back
CLUB: Leicester
NATIONALITY: French

Wesley Fofana became an FA Cup winner and Premier League regular in his first season with Leicester but we're expecting bigger things to come. The defender is already looking like a snip at £36.5m as his composed performances saw him win the Foxes' Young Player of the Year award in 2021.

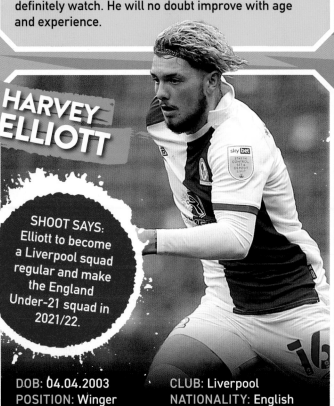
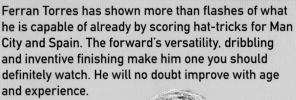

HARVEY ELLIOTT

SHOOT SAYS: Elliott to become a Liverpool squad regular and make the England Under-21 squad in 2021/22.

DOB: 04.04.2003
POSITION: Winger
CLUB: Liverpool
NATIONALITY: English

Harvey Elliott has already hit the headlines in his short career so far by becoming the youngest player to ever play in the Premier League. The talented winger will now be aiming to make a real impact in the top league after an impressive loan spell in the Championship with Blackburn.

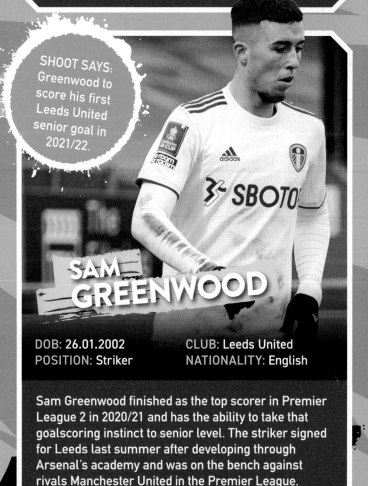

SHOOT SAYS: Greenwood to score his first Leeds United senior goal in 2021/22.

SAM GREENWOOD

DOB: 26.01.2002
POSITION: Striker
CLUB: Leeds United
NATIONALITY: English

Sam Greenwood finished as the top scorer in Premier League 2 in 2020/21 and has the ability to take that goalscoring instinct to senior level. The striker signed for Leeds last summer after developing through Arsenal's academy and was on the bench against rivals Manchester United in the Premier League.

GETTING TO KNOW...

LEWIS DUNK

BRIGHTON & HOVE ALBION

Lewis Dunk is a Brighton & Hove Albion legend having played a key role in his hometown club's rise from League One to the Premier League.

BRIGHTON STAR TACKLES SHOOT'S QUICK FIRE ROUND

Now captain of the Seagulls, Dunk has been capped by England and is one of the top-flight's most consistent centre-backs.

You will already know he is a top defender who is strong off the ball and classy on it, but how much do you really know the Albion ace?

Here Dunk reveals more about himself as he answers Shoot's quick-fire questions.

ARTIST YOU LISTEN TO PRE-MATCH?
DRAKE

CHILDHOOD FOOTBALLING IDOL?
JOHN TERRY

BEST STRIKER YOU'VE PLAYED AGAINST?
SERGIO AGUERO

FAVOURITE POST-MATCH MEAL?
PIZZA

BEST BRIGHTON MOMENT SO FAR?
PROMOTION TO THE PREMIER LEAGUE

FAVOURITE PLACE TO HOLIDAY?
DUBAI

FUNNIEST TEAMMATE?
ME

SMART OR CASUAL?
CASUAL

DREAM CENTRE-BACK PARTNER?
JOHN TERRY

GOAL OR GOAL-LINE CLEARANCE?
GOAL LINE CLEARANCE, LAST MINUTE!

FAVOURITE TV SERIES?
ENTOURAGE

ACTOR TO PLAY YOU IN A FILM ABOUT YOUR LIFE?
BLAKE HARRISON

WORST DRESS SENSE AT BRIGHTON?
AARON CONNOLLY

FAVOURITE SPORT OTHER THAN FOOTBALL?
GOLF

FAVOURITE EVER BRIGHTON KIT?
2019/20 HOME KIT

TEAMMATE YOU'D BE MOST WORRIED TO HAVE AT YOUR HOUSE?
AARON CONNOLLY - HE'S TOO MESSY!

DREAM STREAM

The footballers on a whole new level...

Starring on the big screens from the biggest stadiums, you probably don't imagine the world's greatest footballers kicking back and loading up a video game. But some of the biggest names even have their own personal channels and live stream to thousands of fans. Every player on this list is gaming mad – check them out!

NEYMAR

When he's not bossing the world with his football skills, Neymar regularly streams Fortnite on his own Twitch channel that already has millions of followers. As well as accessing sessions over an hour long, his best short clips and epic moments are readily available too.

TWITCH: neymarjr

MESUT OZIL

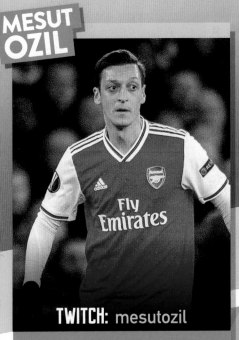

TWITCH: mesutozil

Mesut Ozil is happy to assist you in your evening entertainment, with a stream of Fortnite on his personal Twitch channel. The playmaker has streamed games live with ex-Arsenal teammate Sead Kolasinac, as well as fellow German star Julian Draxler.

DELE ALLI

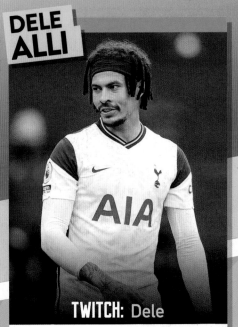

TWITCH: Dele

Dele was also one of the first to really cause a splash when he and Tottenham Hotspur teammates began to jump on Fortnite during its early boom. He started his own Twitch channel playing Call of Duty too, even hosting sponsored competition winners.

TRENT ALEXANDER-ARNOLD

TWITCH: No channel

Okay, so Trent Alexander-Arnold doesn't actually have a channel of his own, but he is an extremely keen FIFA player and often posts about it on his socials. Users have spotted his account online and he even reached the final of the FIFA 20 ePremier League invitational – which Diogo Jota won.

SERGIO AGUERO

TWITCH: SLAKUN10

Barcelona striker Sergio Aguero streams loads of different games on his Twitch channel, including Grand Theft Auto, Valorant and sometimes just spends time talking in front of the camera with followers. The Argentine ace has even called Lionel Messi while streaming just for a chat.

DAVID MEYLER

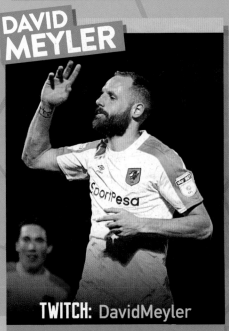

TWITCH: DavidMeyler

Although technically a retired pro now, the former Hull City man deserves to be on this list as one of the originals. David Meyler streams FIFA and Call of Duty on his Twitch channel but has also been a regular YouTube star, collaborating with the likes of FIFA favourite Bateson87.

DIOGO JOTA

TWITCH: DiogoJotaEsports

Liverpool's Diogo Jota is really quite unbelievable at FIFA. Jota regularly streams the football game with insane success, even going 30-0 and finishing 1st in the entire world during a round of the highly competitive FUT Champions Weekend League.

RECORD SCORER

These super strikers are all-time leading scorers at major clubs. But can you match each player to the record number of goals they scored?

 **A** SERGIO AGUERO

 **B** WAYNE ROONEY

 **C** THIERRY HENRY

 **D** FRANK LAMPARD

 **211**

 **253**

 **260**

 **228**

GROUND SIZE

Match these clubs to how many fans their stadium can seat...

 **A** West Ham United

 **B** Newcastle United

 **C** Liverpool

 **D** Leeds United

52,354 **54,074** **37,890** **60,000**

Answers on page 77

SPOT THE EIGHT

Think you have the vision of Bruno Fernandes?
Spot the eight differences in these photos below. Circle each one you find...

EURO STARS

Match the player to the country they represented at Euro 2020.

A OLEKSANDR ZINCHENKO

B ADAMA TRAORE

C GIANLUIGI DONNARUMMA

D DAVID ALABA

AUSTRIA _____

ITALY _____

SPAIN _____

UKRAINE _____

Answers on page 77

JAMES ARTHUR

James Arthur has become one of the biggest names in UK music since winning the 2012 edition of hit show the X Factor. But the chart-topping star's biggest passion away from the stage and recording studio is football. The son of an English mother and Scottish father, the singer-songwriter's club loyalty is split firmly down the middle. Shoot sat down with the multi-platinum artist to talk about his love for the beautiful game.

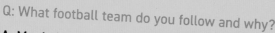

Q: What football team do you follow and why?

A: My dad is a Rangers nut and has tried to make me a fan since I was a kid but I support Middlesbrough as well. I'm from Boro and a lot of my friends support them too.

Q: What are your earliest footballing memories?

A: My dad brought me up watching the golden era of Rangers football. He has all the tapes so I was watching players like Ally McCoist, Gazza and Mark Hateley scoring great goals. So seeing those Rangers tapes at that time was part of my early footballing education.

Q: How was it training with Rangers when Ally McCoist was manager in 2014?

A: It was really surreal because I was midway through a tour and suddenly my manager said that I'm going to play football with Ally McCoist. I got to kick a ball around with him and the rest of the team which was a very proud moment. I had a couple of nice touches during the session but just missed out on a contract.

Q: Who were your favourite players growing up?

A: For Rangers I would have to say Gazza and the legend, Ally McCoist. Then for Middlesbrough my favourite player growing up was Juninho. I had the pleasure of watching him play live a couple of times and I just thought he was an unbelievable player.

Q: Favourite current players and why?

A: I love Paul Pogba. He divides opinion but he just has the ability to show a bit of class to take hold of a game. I also like Jack Grealish because he is positive minded and always looking to undo the opposition. Kevin De Bruyne is another as he has vision that other players just don't have. Then of course I can't leave out the great Lionel Messi and Cristiano Ronaldo.

Q: How great was it to see Rangers win their first Scottish Premiership title in 10 years last season?

A: The club have had a tough decade and it's been a long time rebuilding. They've had to sit back and watch Celtic dominate the league but when Steven Gerrard came in he just transformed the team and got them ticking. It's been amazing seeing them make a comeback, win the title and win it in style. They've been playing good football for a couple of years now and absolutely dominated last season.

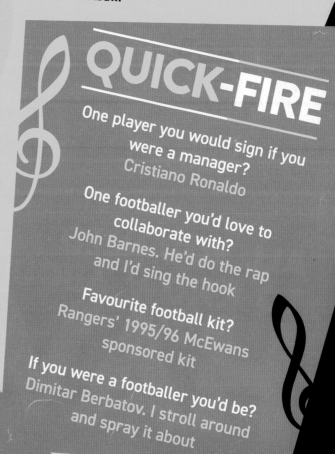

Q: What do you expect from Rangers and Boro in the 2021/22 season?

A: It's important for Rangers to lay down a marker now and create their own era by keeping hold of the title for a couple of years. With Middlesbrough it's such a tough league and is very hard to predict what we're going to do. But I do like Neil Warnock and with his record in the Championship he could be the man to get us into the play-offs.

Q: Do you watch a lot of football?

A: It's always on in my house. Although my teams are Middlesbrough and Rangers I'm just a huge football fan in general and will go to any game I get the chance to go to. Because I live down south I've been to Spurs, Chelsea and other grounds. I just love football.

QUICK-FIRE

One player you would sign if you were a manager?
Cristiano Ronaldo

One footballer you'd love to collaborate with?
John Barnes. He'd do the rap and I'd sing the hook

Favourite football kit?
Rangers' 1995/96 McEwans sponsored kit

If you were a footballer you'd be?
Dimitar Berbatov. I stroll around and spray it about

STAR STAT!
Havertz became Bayer Leverkusen's youngest ever Bundesliga player when he made his debut at the age of 17 years and 126 days.

Havertz missed Leverkusen's 2017/18 Champions League last-16 tie against Atletico Madrid because he was still studying.

DOB:
11.06.1999
AACHEN, GERMANY

ALL YOU NEED TO KNOW ABOUT...
HAVERTZ

FACT FILE

3 FAMOUS MANAGERS:

JOACHIM LOW (Germany)
PETER BOSZ (Bayer Leverkusen)
THOMAS TUCHEL (Chelsea)

QUIZ QUESTION:

Which club did Havertz score his first Premier League goal against?

A: Aston Villa
B: Everton
C: Southampton

Answer on page 77

3 FAMOUS TEAMMATES:

N'GOLO KANTE (Chelsea)
TONI KROOS (Germany)
JOSHUA KIMMICH (Germany)

INTERNATIONAL:

TEAM: Germany
DEBUT: vs Peru (9 September 2018)
FIRST GOAL: vs Argentina (9 October 2019)

TRANSFER FEES:

SEPTEMBER 2020 – Bayer Leverkusen to Chelsea – £62m
COMBINED TRANSFER FEE: £62M

HONOURS:

CLUB: Champions League

INDIVIDUAL: Bundesliga Team of the Season, Bundesliga Player of the Month x 2, UEFA Champions League Breakthrough XI, UEFA Europa League Squad of the Season.

SENIOR CAREER TIMELINE:

Bayer Leverkusen 2016-2020

Chelsea 2020-present

MARCUS RASHFORD

Marcus Rashford leads the way when it comes to footballers as a driving force for positive change. The England striker campaigned for the government to allow 1.3m children to claim free school meal vouchers in England's summer holidays during the coronavirus pandemic. As an ambassador for FareShare, his efforts also triggered an estimated £20m of additional donations to children who need food the most. Rashford was recognised for his work by being awarded an MBE in the Queen's Birthday Honours list.

FOOTBALL UNITED

The players giving back in a time of need...

Footballers have been stepping up and using their fame to drive positive change for people in what has been a difficult time. We take a look at just a handful of players (there are too many to name!) who have made a real heartwarming difference to others over the last 12 months.

RYAN YATES

Nottingham Forest midfielder Ryan Yates is among many EFL players who started delivering food parcel donations to locals who needed it most. The EFL community response has seen over 1m food parcels, 150,000+ pieces of PPE and 22,000+ essential prescriptions delivered during the pandemic.

WILFRIED ZAHA

Ivory Coast international Wilfried Zaha offered to open up 50 of his properties in London to NHS staff, following the coronavirus outbreak by sharing a post from co-owner Obi Williams and urging health workers online to 'reach out'. On top of that, he also donates 10% of his wages every month to charity.

NEYMAR

Neymar donated around £800,000 to aid the battle against Covid. The PSG star split his donation between UNICEF and a fund created in his homeland of Brazil. Best of all he did this privately because he did not want to take the credit for it, but the media found out and now the whole world knows the forward did a good deed.

ANDREW ROBERTSON

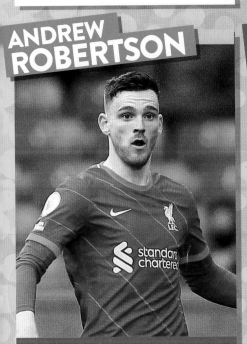

Liverpool star Andy Robertson made huge donations to six different foodbanks in his hometown of Glasgow, helping them to survive and supply thousands of meals to the hungry during the pandemic. The Scotland captain is hugely generous but extremely humble.

PATRICK BAMFORD

Patrick Bamford donated £5,000 to a local primary school in January 2021. The money funded iPads in order to ensure each pupil could access online learning when schools were closed. He also sent a personal video message, urging the kids to keep working hard.

PEP GUARDIOLA

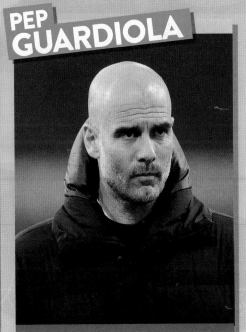

Pep Guardiola helped out in his home country by donating £920,000 to Spain in the fight against the disease. The Man City boss' funds provided medical equipment and protective material for hospital staff. Pep certainly produced the goods both in and out of the dugout in 2021.

PG 9 - STAR SPELLER

Rashford
Soucek
Salah
Hojbjerg
Cantwell
Eze
Smith Rowe
Mahrez
Azpilicueta
Calvert-Lewin
Iheanacho

Score: / 11

PG 10-11 - SO YOU THINK YOU KNOW... PHIL FODEN?

1. FALSE
2. FALSE
3. TRUE
4. FALSE
5. TRUE
6. TRUE
7. FALSE
8. TRUE
9. FALSE
10. TRUE

Score: / 10

PG 16 - MILESTONE MOMENTS

1. Sadio Mane (E)
2. Harry Kane (B)
3. Youri Tielemans (D)
4. Joe Willock (C)
5. Sergio Aguero (G)
6. Conor Coady (H)
7. Patrick Bamford (A)
8. Seamus Coleman (F)

Score: / 8

PG 17 - THE AGE GAME

A. Paul Pogba - 1993
B. James Ward-Prowse - 1994
C. Kasper Schmeichel - 1986
D. Jude Bellingham - 2003
E. Ismaila Sarr - 1998
F. Max Aarons - 2000
G. Robert Sanchez - 1997
H. Thiago Silva - 1984

Score: / 8

PG 24-25 - ALL YOU NEED TO KNOW ABOUT... THIAGO

Quiz Question Answer:
C - Volleyball

Score: / 1

PG 26-27 - SPOT THE STARS

Score: / 8

PG 32 - FIRST CLUB

Gareth Bale – Southampton (D)
Pierre-Emerick Aubameyang - AC Milan (A)
Sadio Mane - FC Metz (E)
Aymeric Laporte - Basconia (B)
James Maddison - Coventry City (F)
Chris Smalling - Maidstone United (C)

Score: / 6

PG 33 - LAST CLUB

Peter Crouch - Burnley (F)
Robin van Persie - Feyenoord (B)
Thierry Henry - New York Red Bulls (A)
Yaya Toure - Qingdao Huanghai FC (E)
Frank Lampard - New York City FC (C)
Patrice Evra – West Ham United (D)

Score: / 6

PG 38 - CLUB CAREER
1. Hakim Ziyech
2. Jamie Vardy
3. Che Adams
4. James Tarkowski
5. Edinson Cavani
6. Lucas Digne

Score: / 6

PG 39 - LEGENDARY LINK-UP
Ledley King - Tottenham (A)
Duncan Ferguson - Everton (E)
Ian Rush - Liverpool (H)
Bobby Moore - West Ham (G)
David Beckham - Manchester United (B)
Luther Blissett - Watford (D)
David Seaman - Arsenal (F)
Didier Drogba – Chelsea (C)

Score: / 6

PG 42 – EFL CHALLENGE
Championship: Birmingham City / Huddersfield Town / Millwall
League One: Accrington Stanley / Ipswich Town / Sunderland
League Two: Bristol Rovers / Oldham Athletic / Salford City

Score: / 9

PG 43 – WHO AM I?
A. Eberechi Eze
B. Kalvin Phillips
C. Fabinho
D. Harry Maguire

Score: / 4

TOTAL SCORE
/244

PG 44-45 – QUIZ OF THE YEAR: POINTS BUILDER
1. Raheem Sterling
2. Japan
3. Kai Havertz
4. Romelu Lukaku
5. Croatia
6. Third
7. Villarreal
8. Italy
9. Sarina Wiegman
10. Derby County
11. Brentford
12. Sam Kerr
13. 2011
14. Birmingham City
15. Yellow

Score: / 120

PG 52-53 - SO YOU THINK YOU KNOW... BUKAYO SAKA?
1. TRUE
2. FALSE
3. TRUE
4. TRUE
5. FALSE
6. FALSE
7. TRUE
8. TRUE
9. TRUE
10. FALSE

Score: / 10

PG 60-61 - SO YOU THINK YOU KNOW... THE WSL?
1. TRUE
2. FALSE
3. FALSE
4. FALSE
5. TRUE
6. FALSE
7. TRUE
8. FALSE
9. TRUE
10. TRUE

Score: / 10

PG 68 – RECORD SCORER
A. Sergio Aguero – 260
B. Wayne Rooney – 253
C. Thierry Henry – 228
D. Frank Lampard– 211

Score: / 4

PG 68 – GROUND SIZE
A. West Ham (London Stadium) – 60,000
B. Newcastle United (St James' Park) - 52,354
C. Liverpool (Anfield) – 54,074
D. Leeds United (Elland Road) – 37,890

Score: / 4

PG 69 – SPOT THE EIGHT

Score: / 8

PG 69 – EURO STARS
A. Oleksandr Zinchenko - Ukraine
B. Adama Traore - Spain
C. Gianluigi Donnarumma - Italy
D. David Alaba - Austria

Score: / 4

PG 72-73 - ALL YOU NEED TO KNOW ABOUT... KAI HAVERTZ
Quiz Question Answer:
C - Southampton

Score: / 1

VISIT SHOOT.CO.UK
NOW THE VOICE OF FOOTBALL ONLINE

For the latest football news, interviews, transfer gossip, stats and much more.

OVER 2.5 MILLION VISITORS PER YEAR!

(Information/figures correct as of: July 2021)